Tattoo Coloring Book For Adults

An Adult Colouring Book of Traditional and Old School Tattoo Designs

Grahame David Garlick

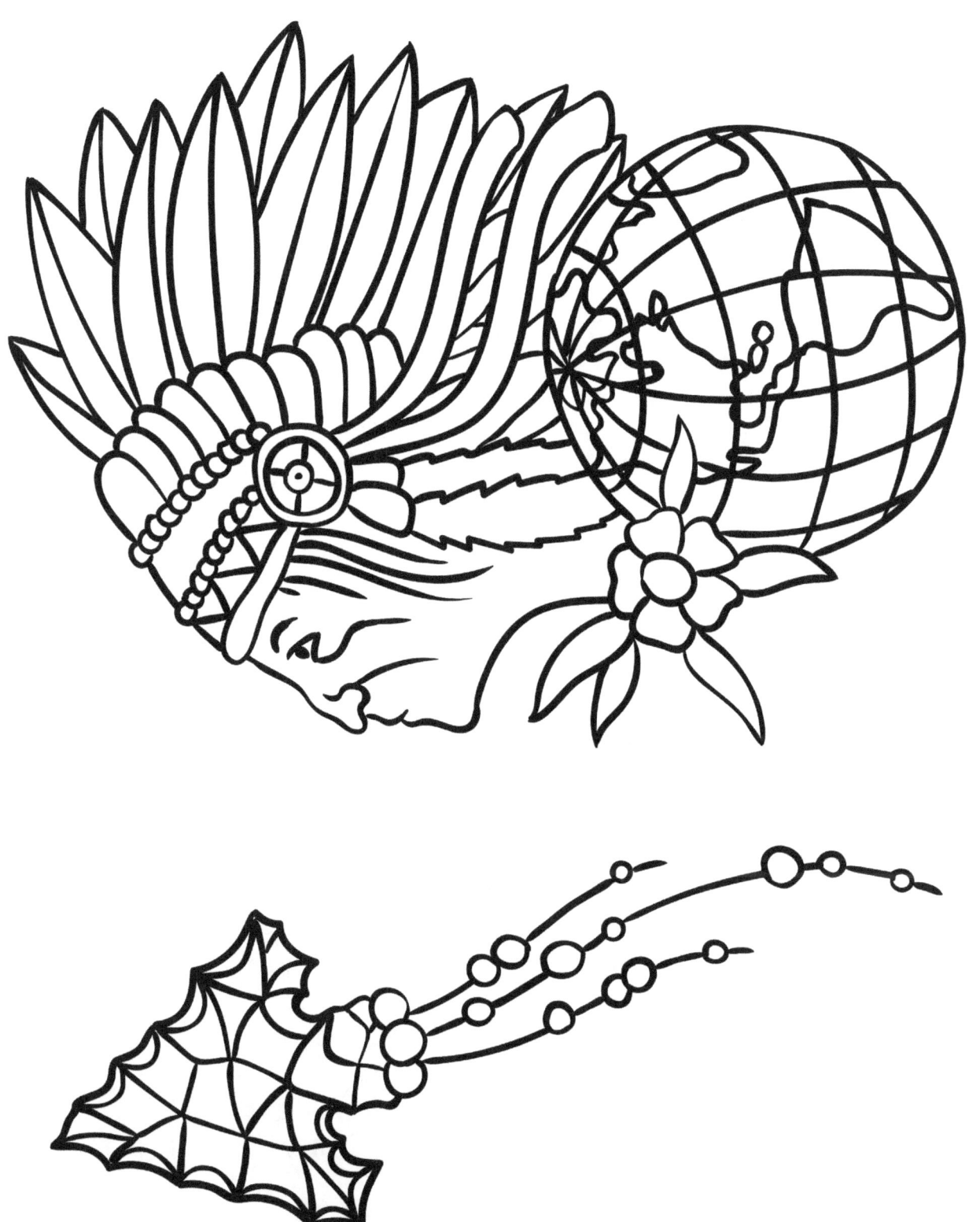

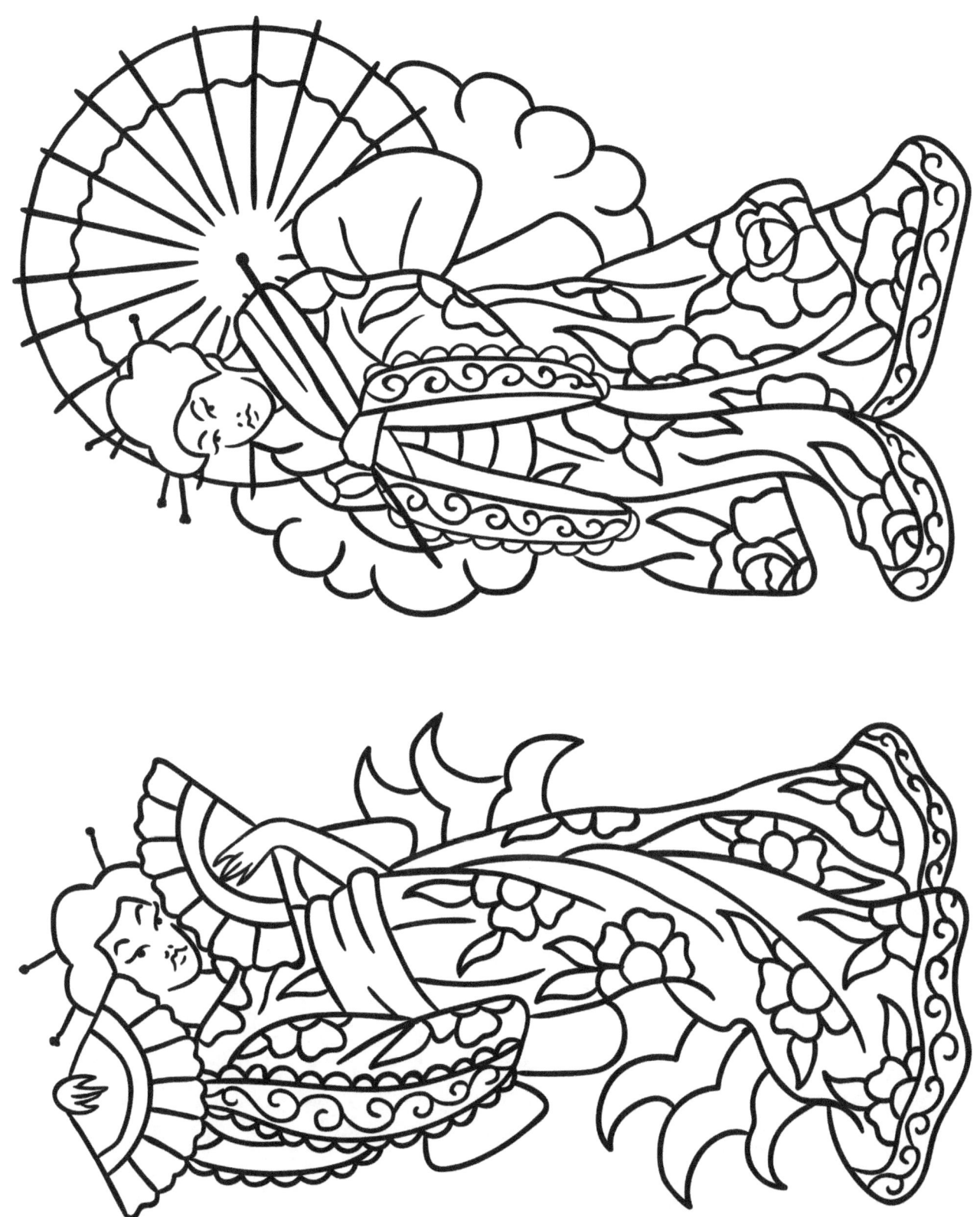

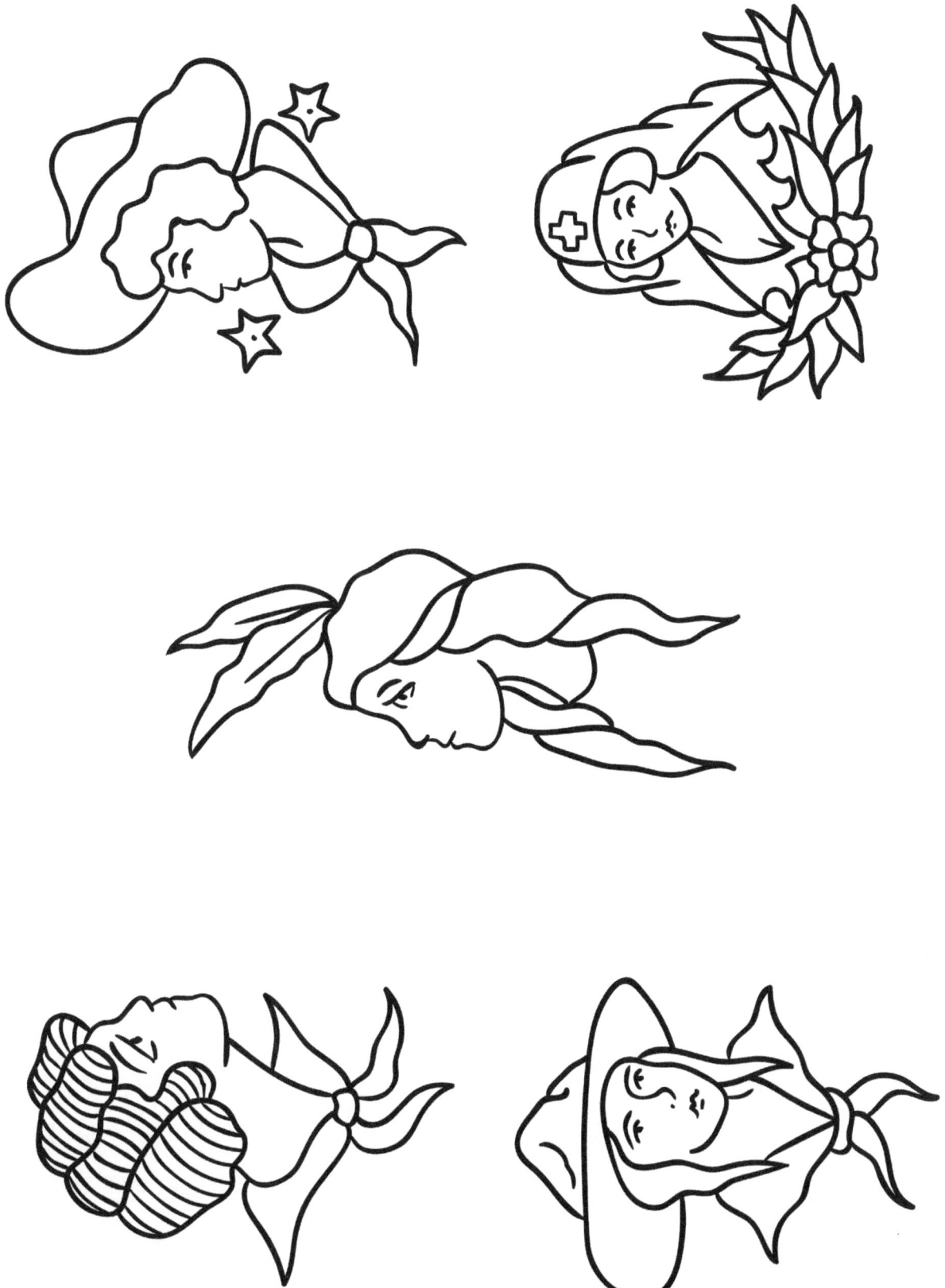

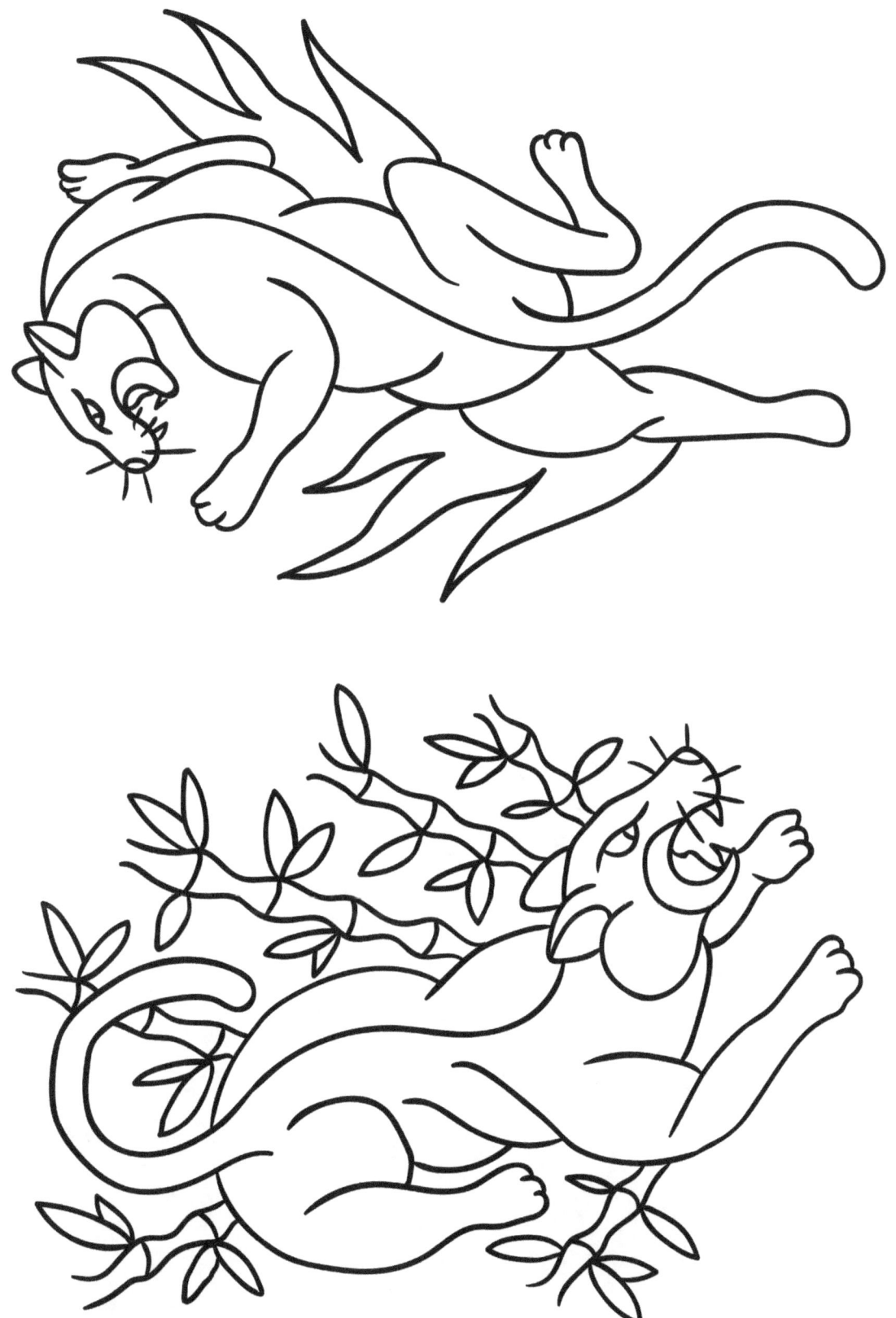

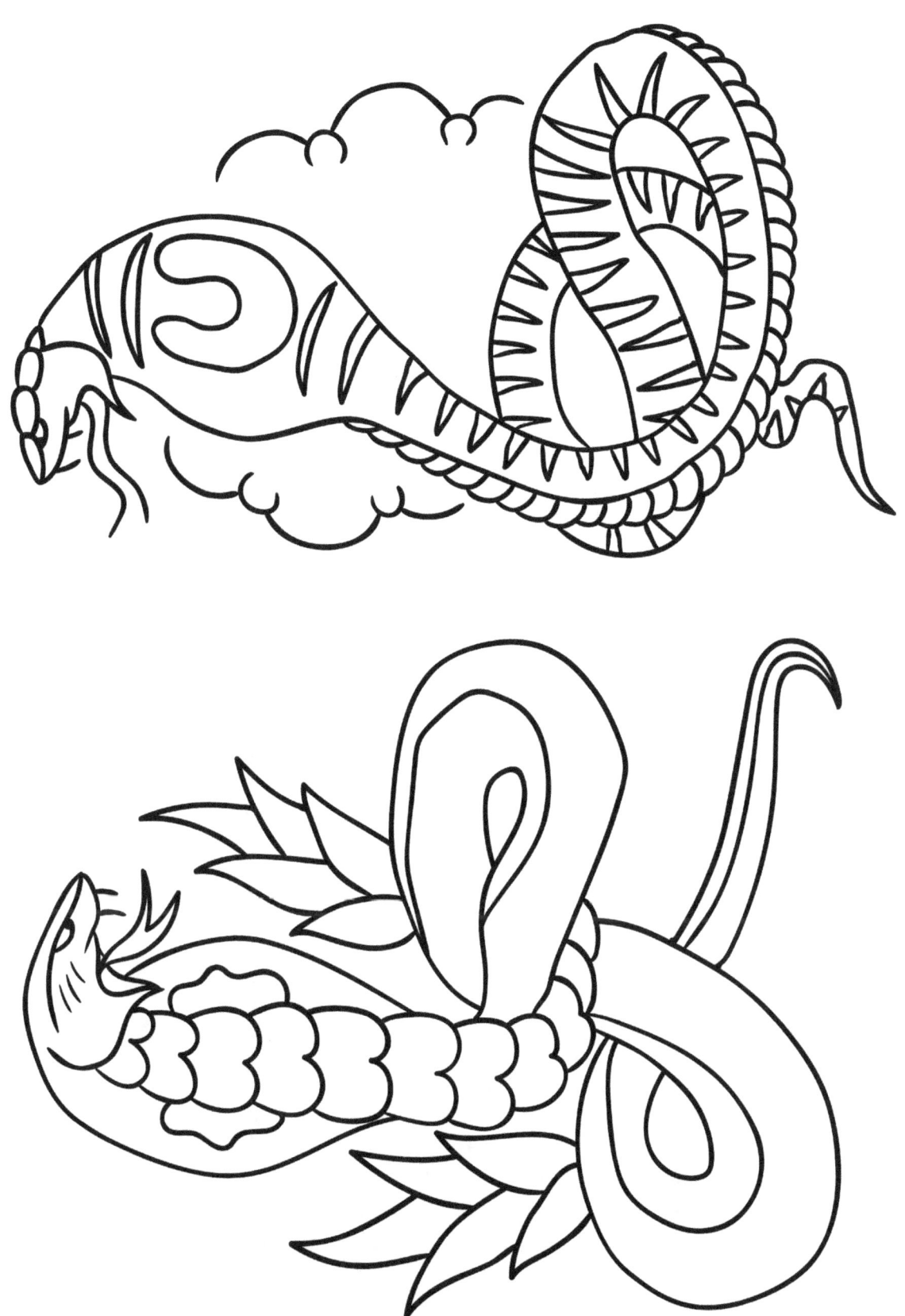

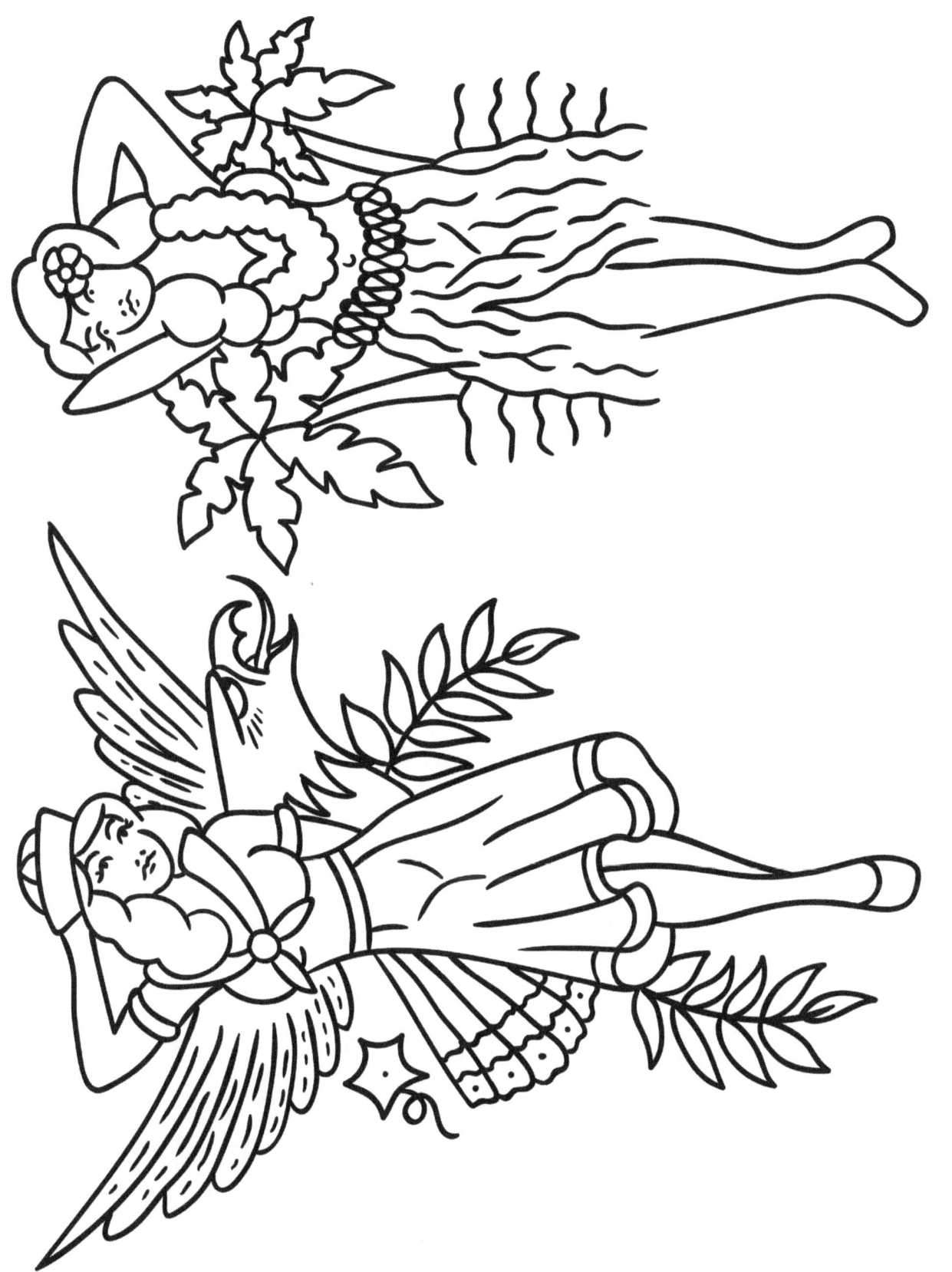

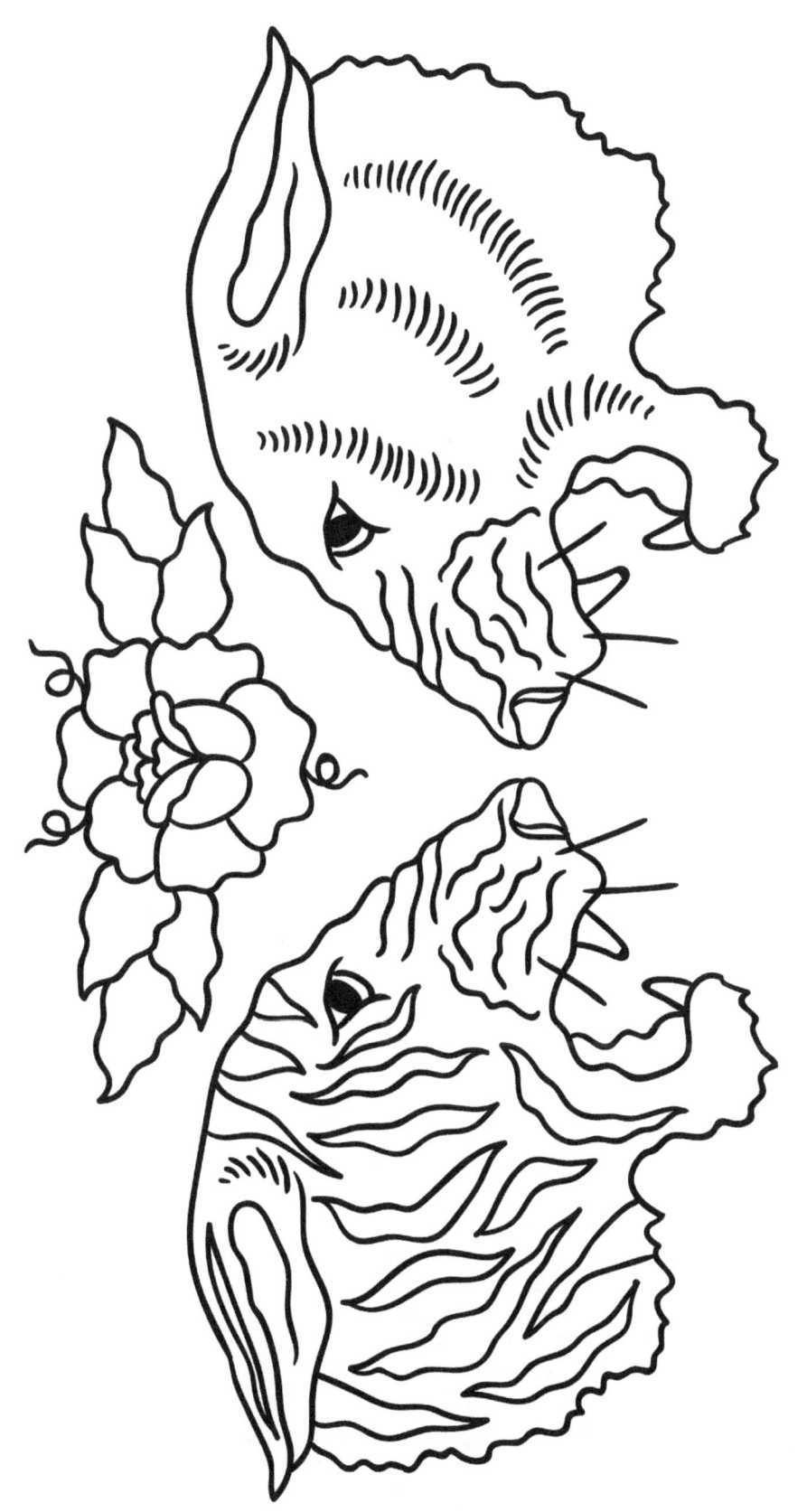

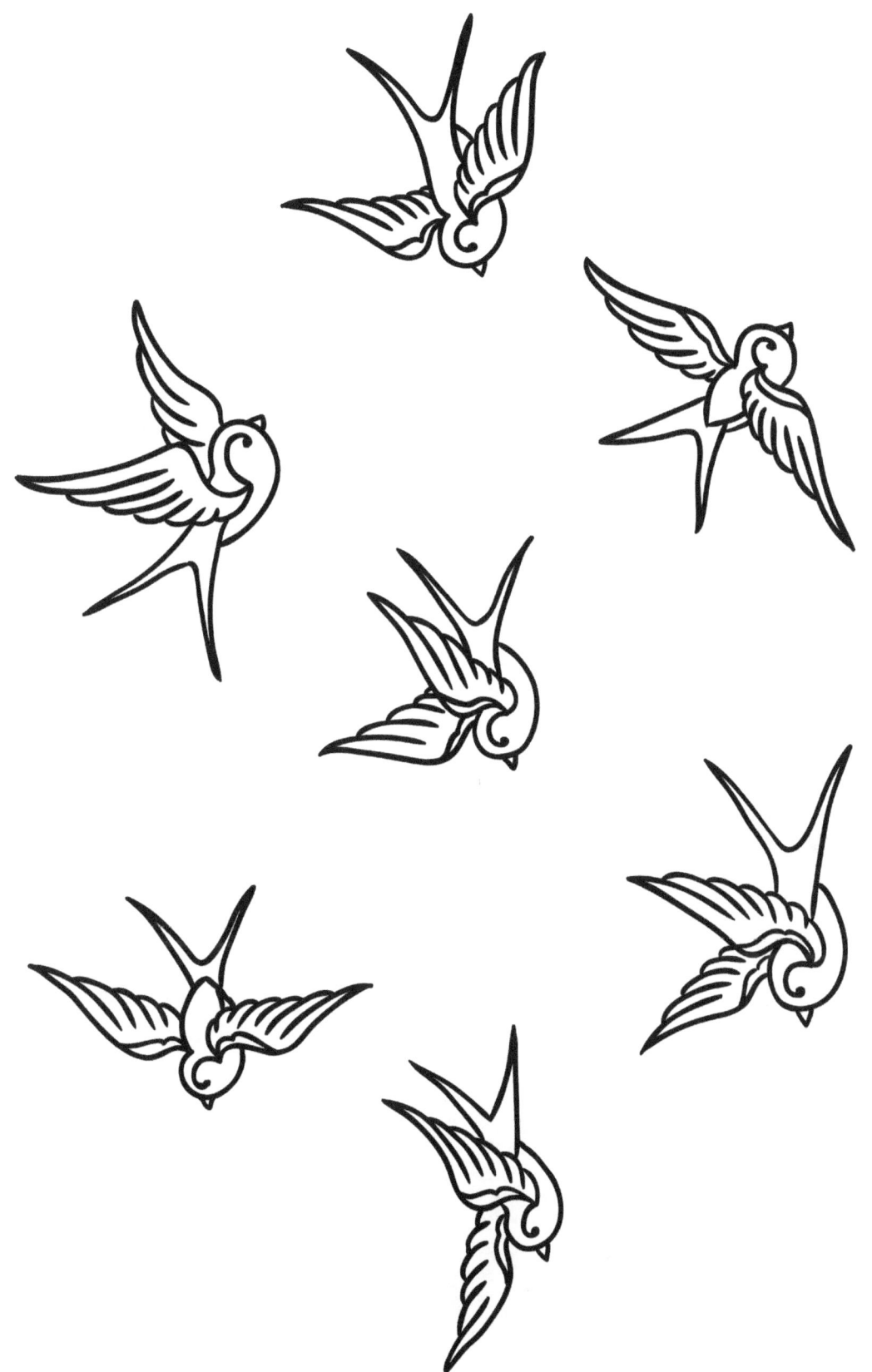

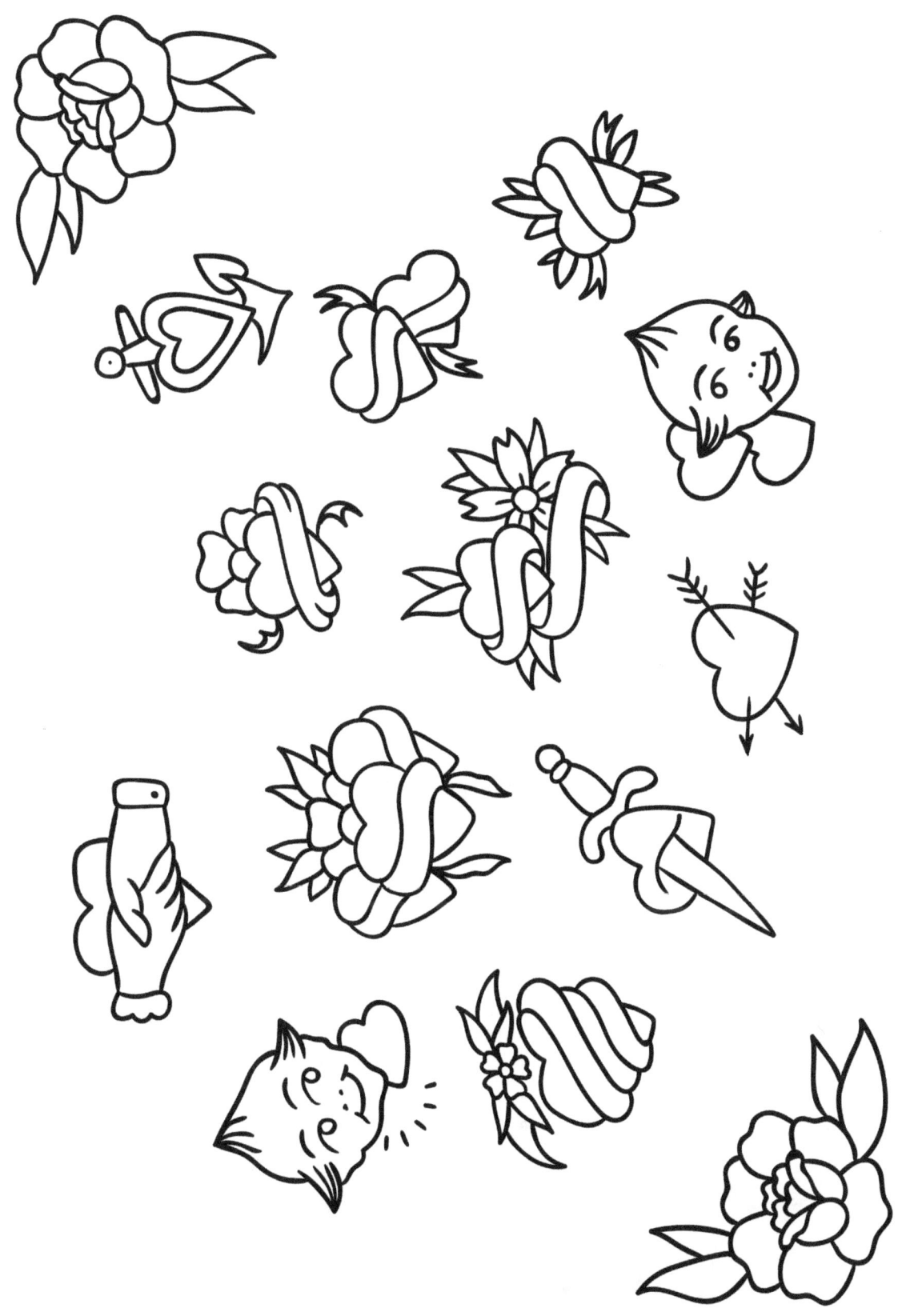

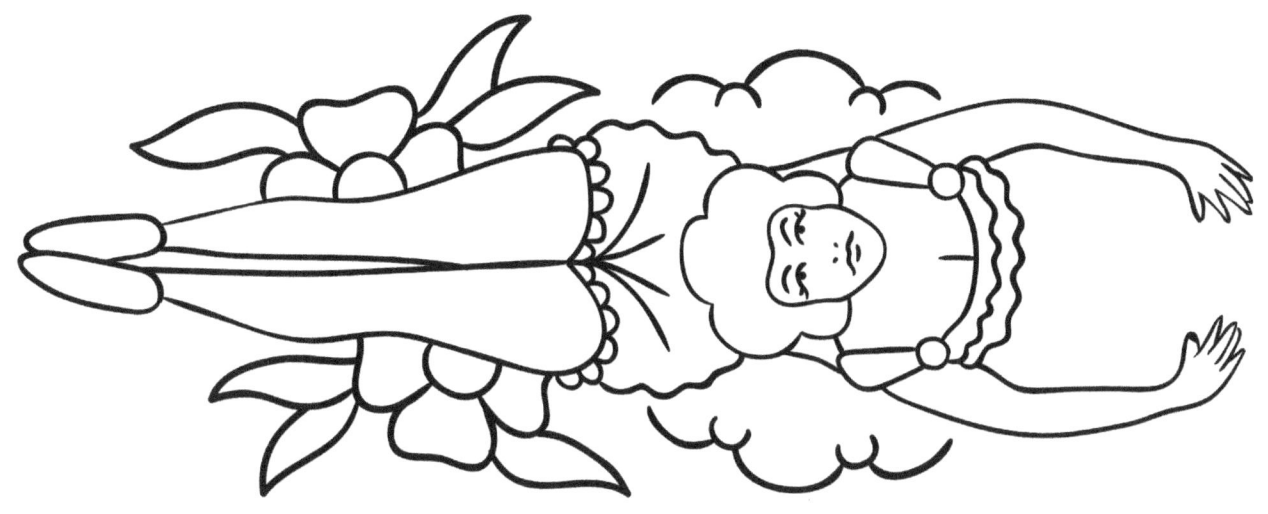

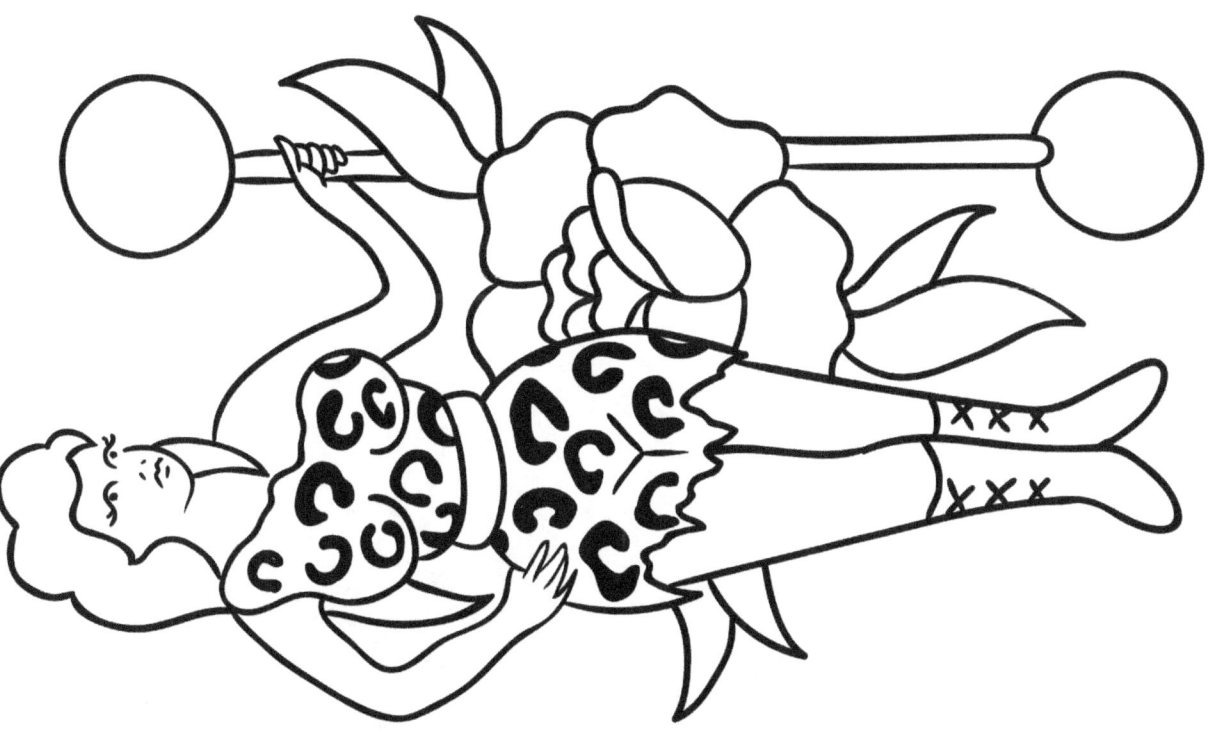

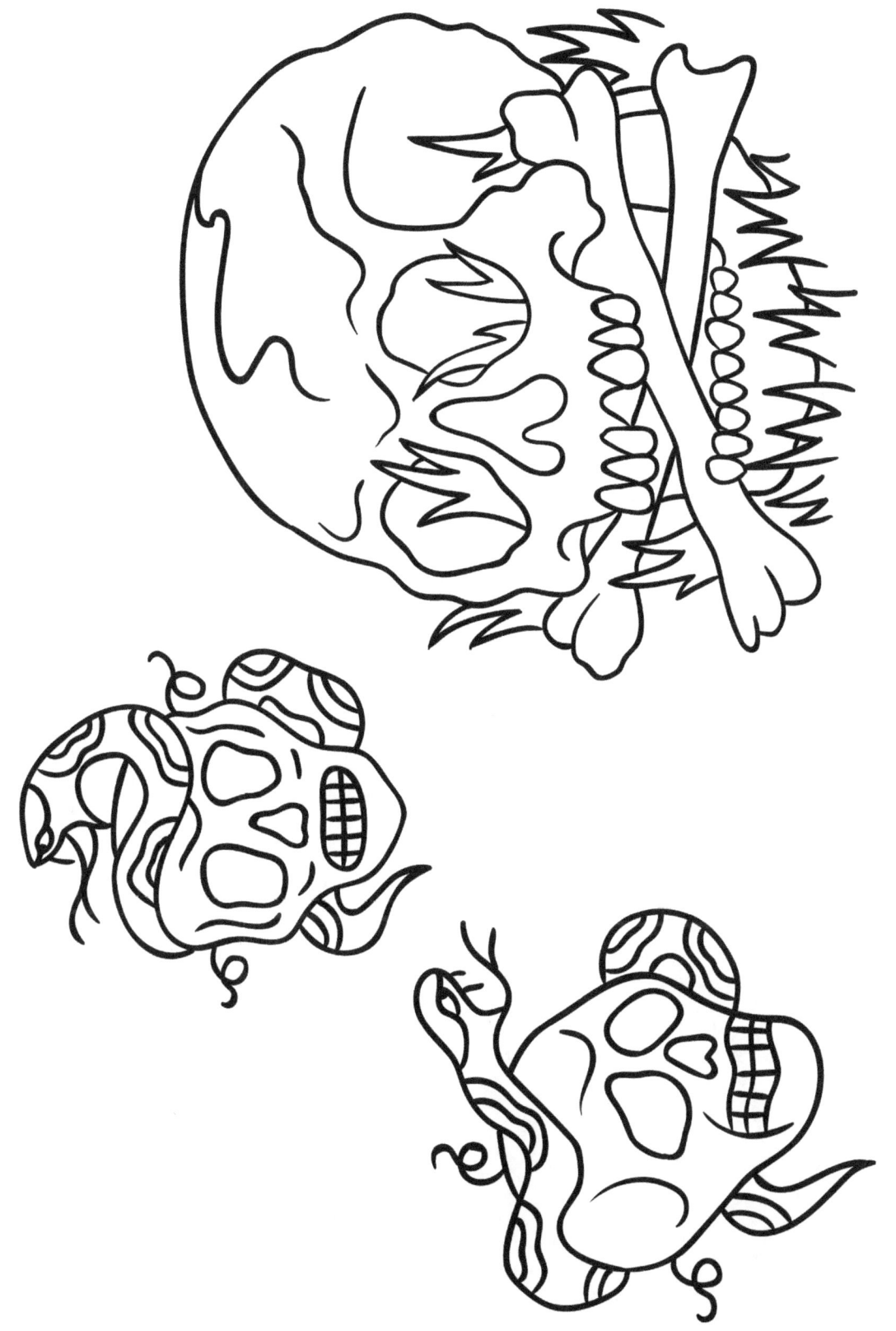

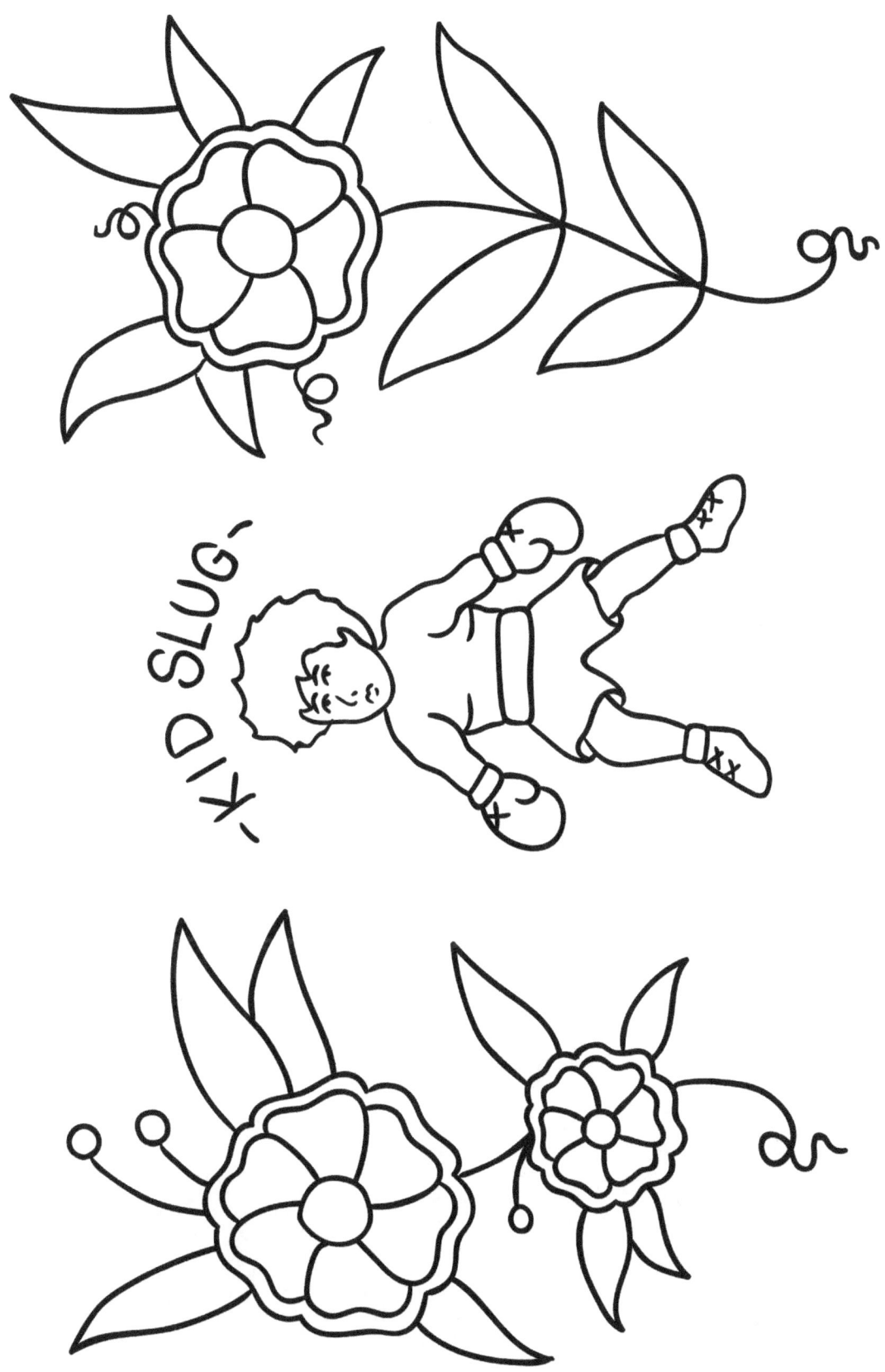

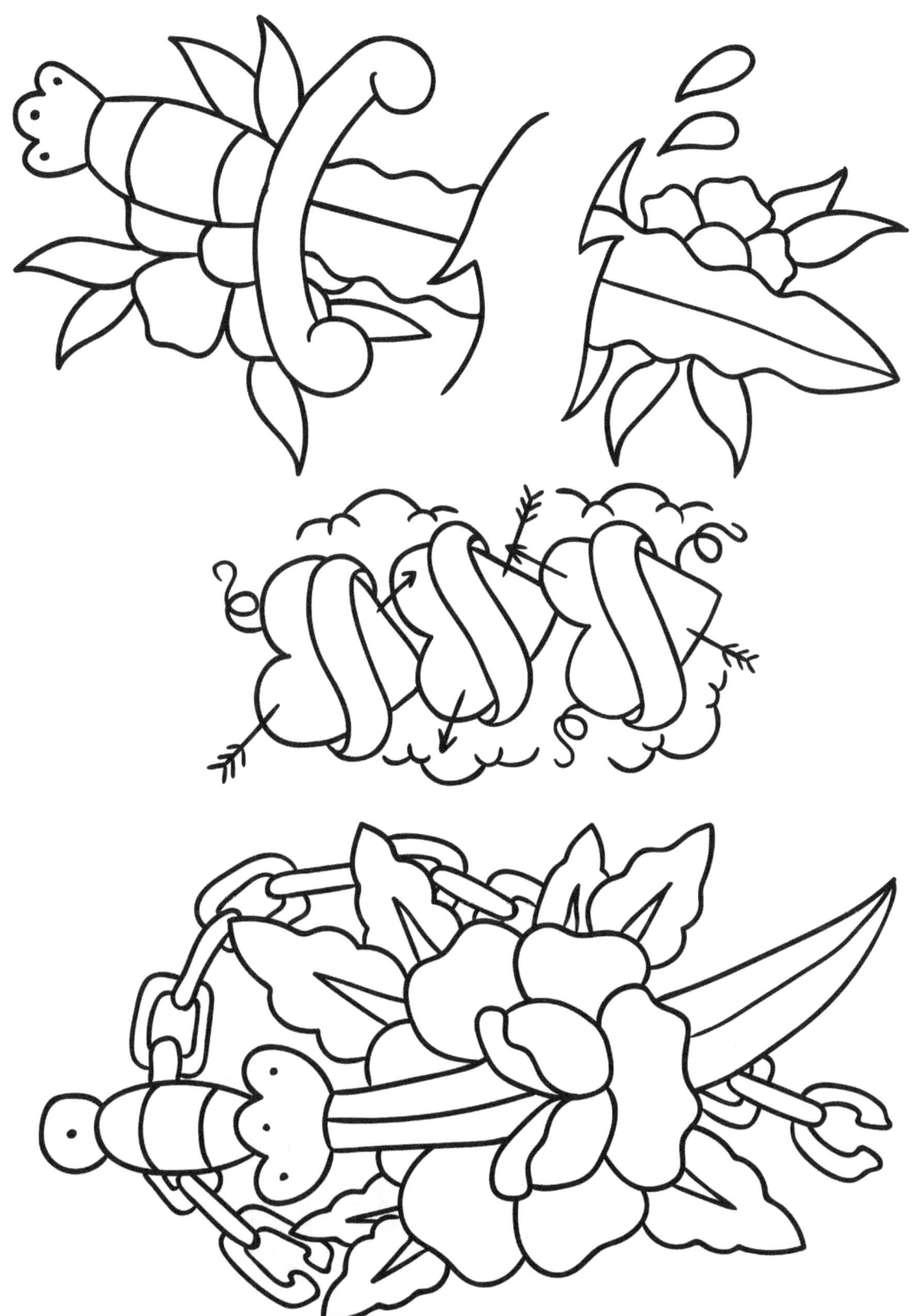

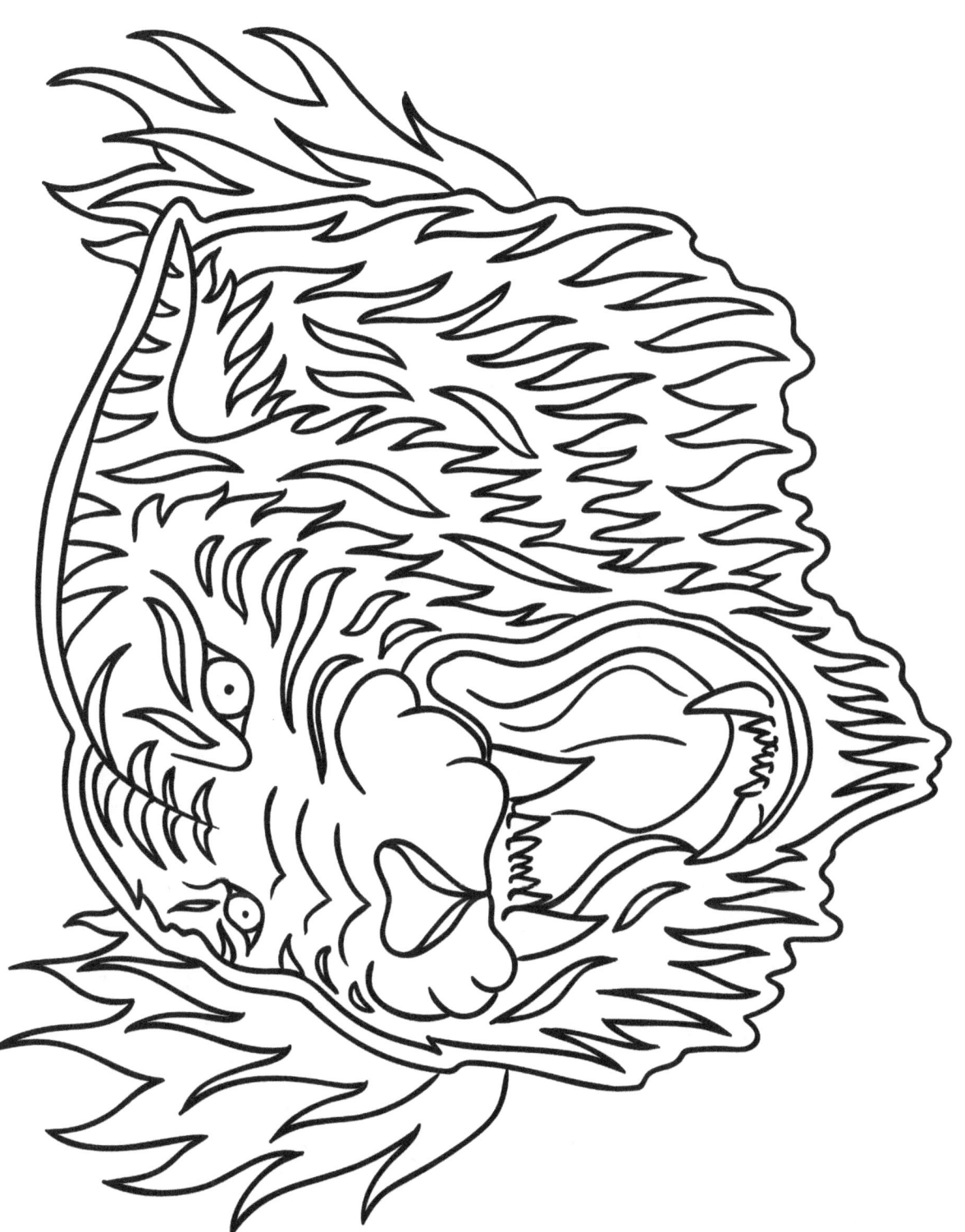

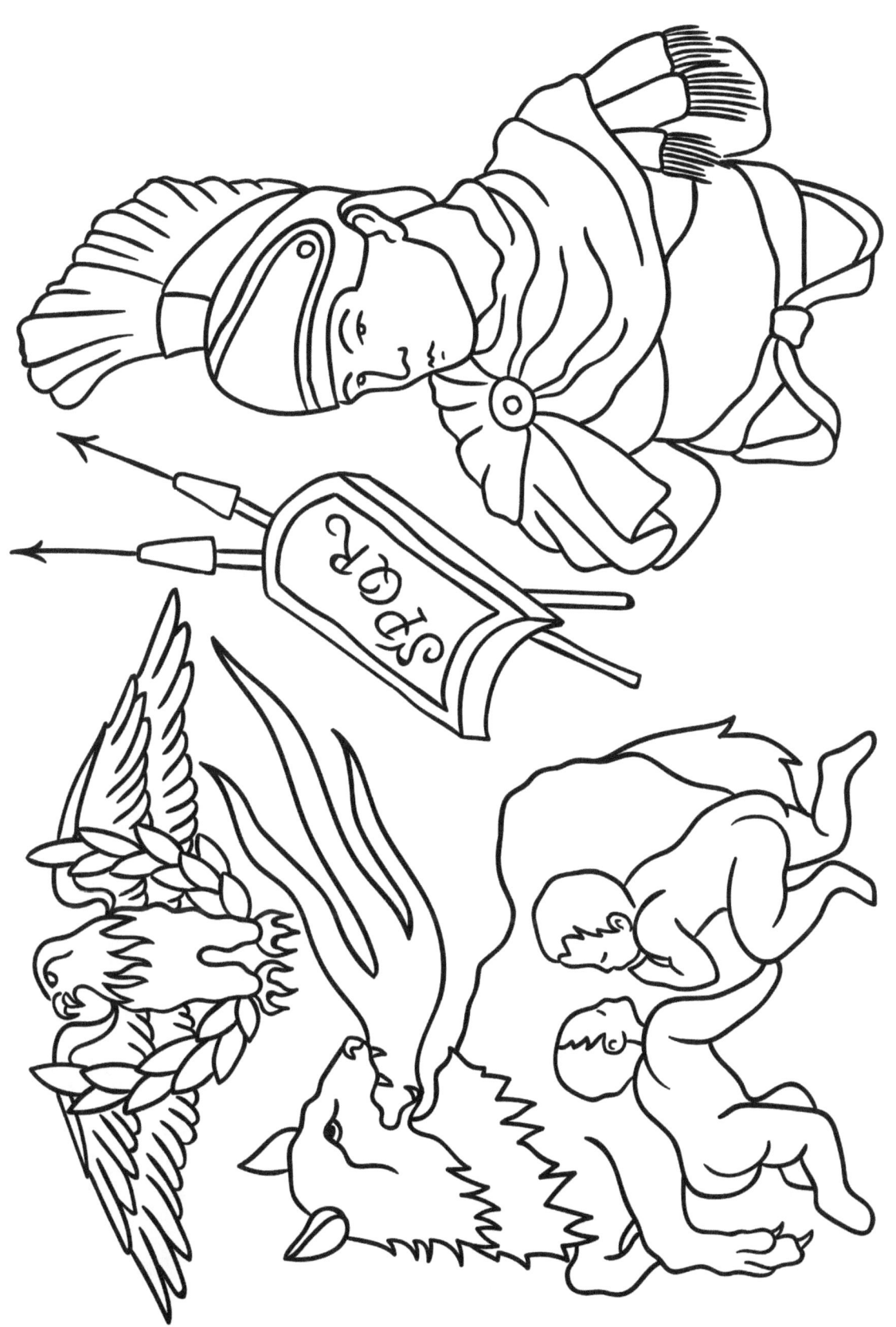

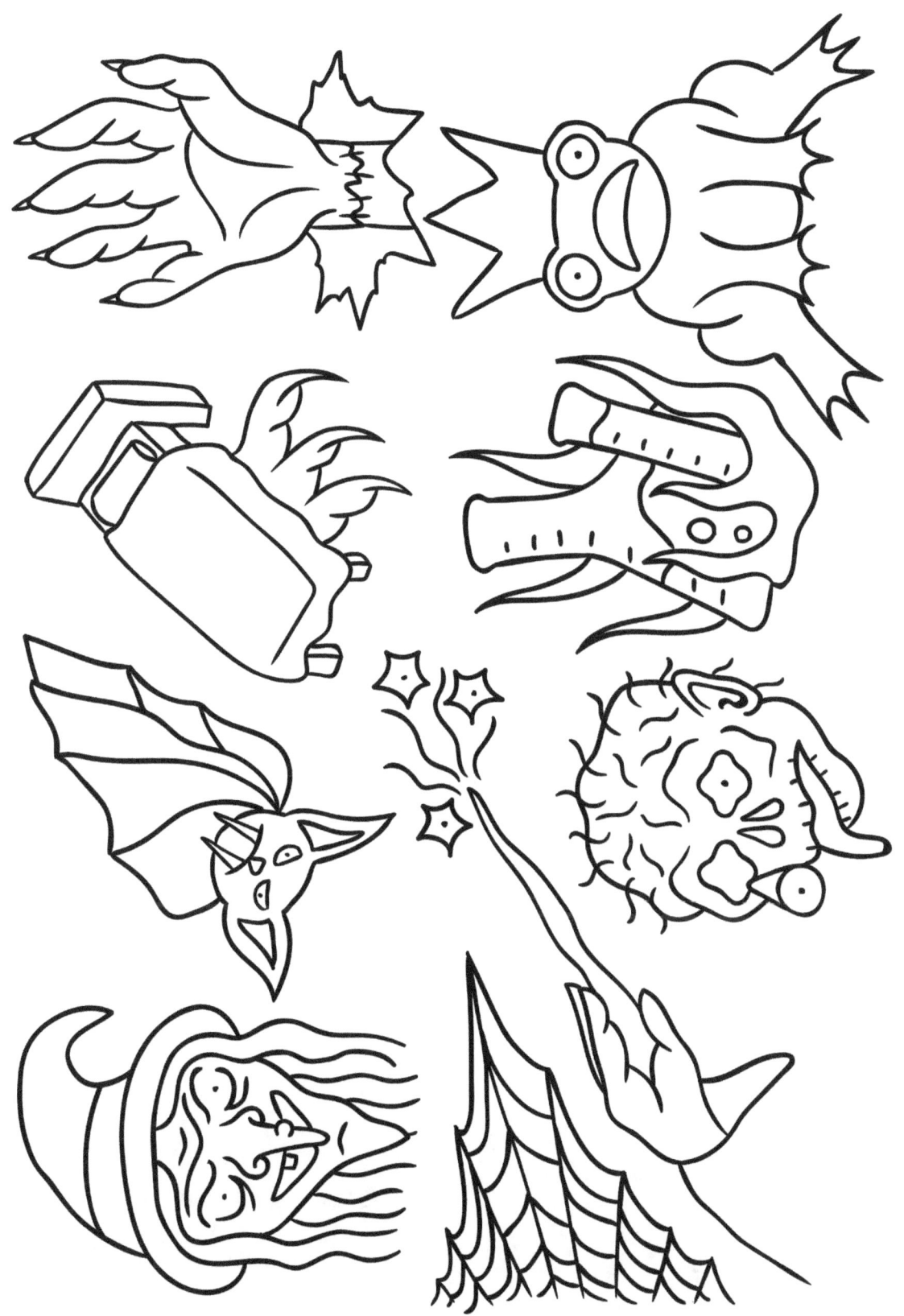

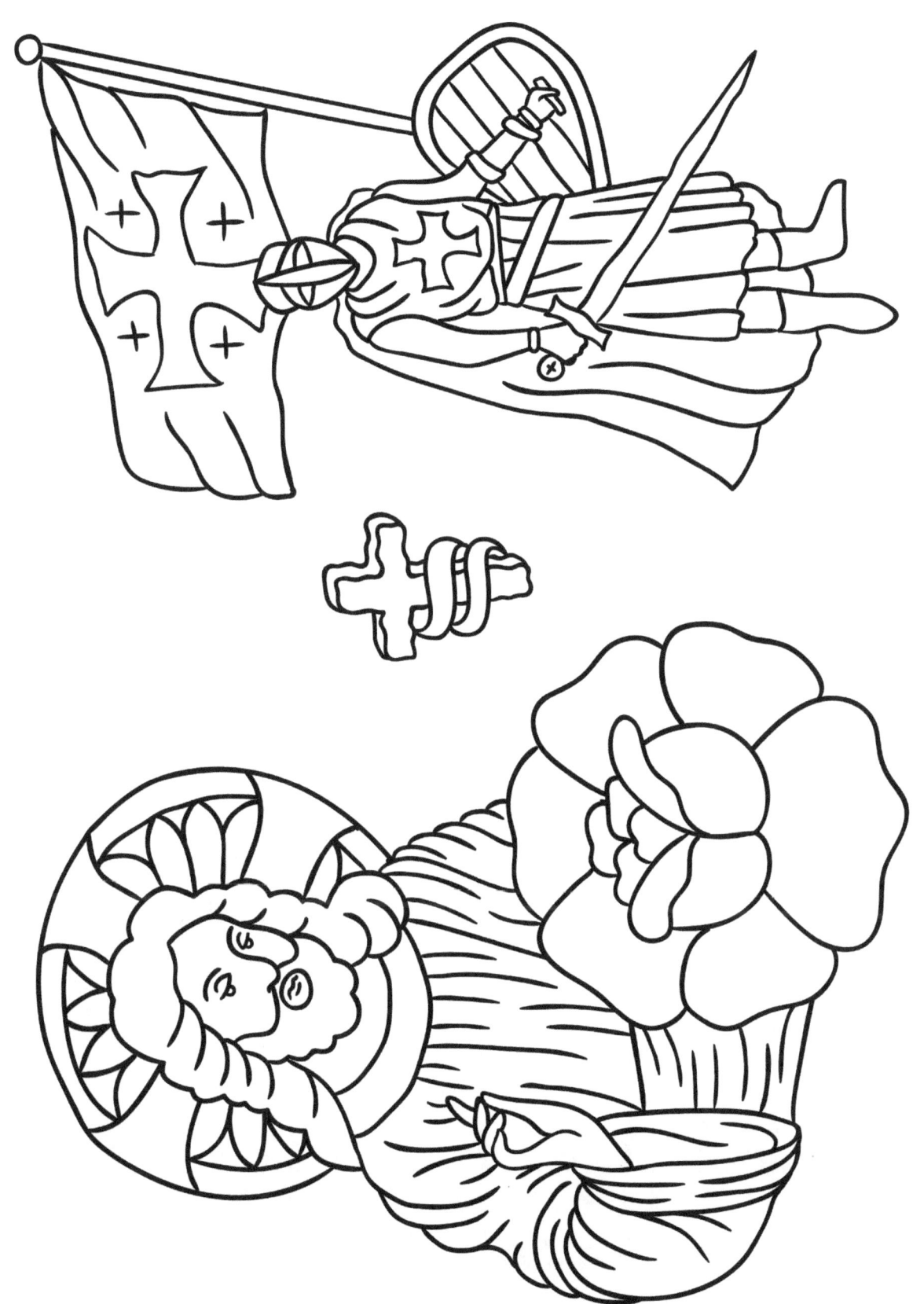

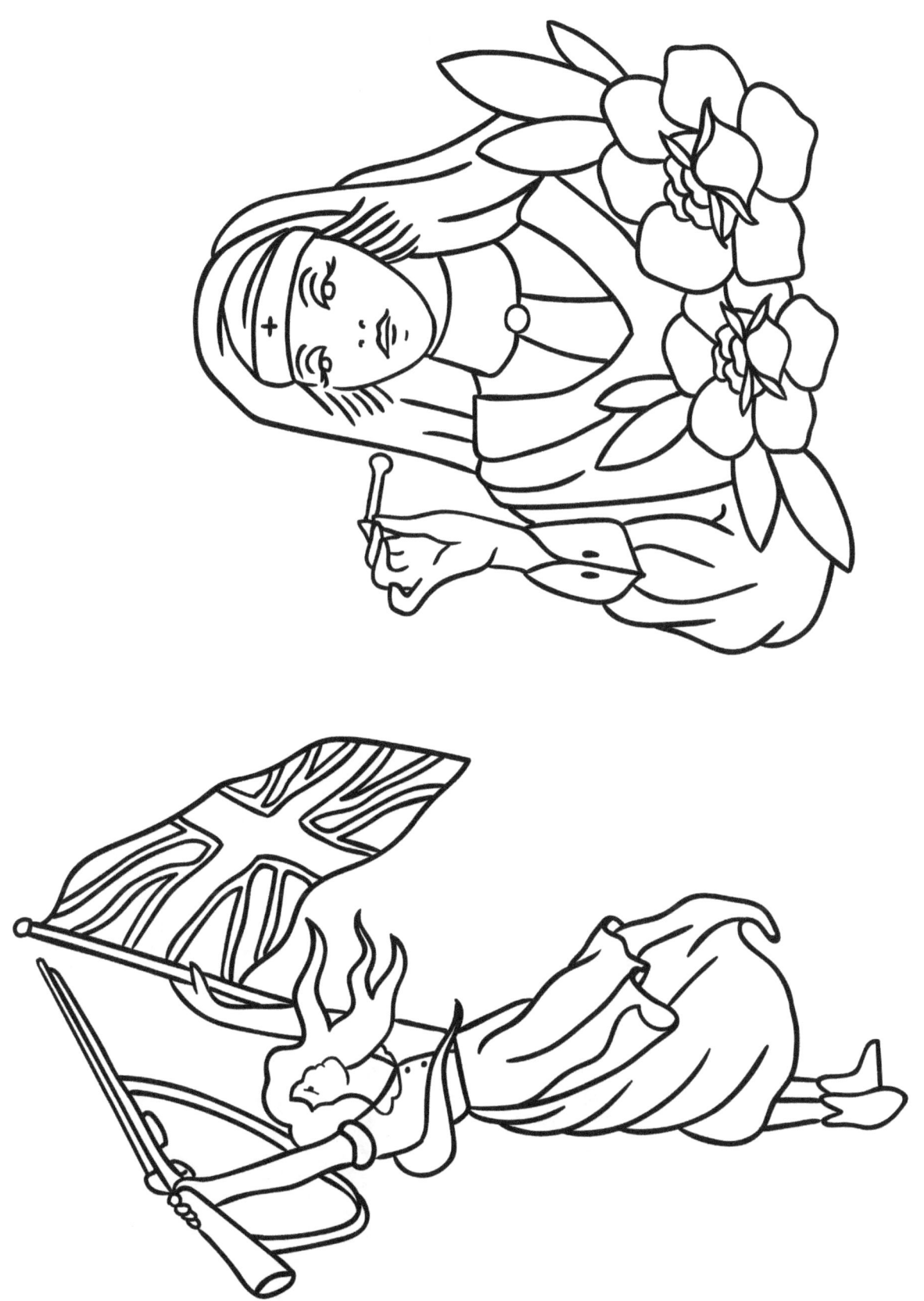

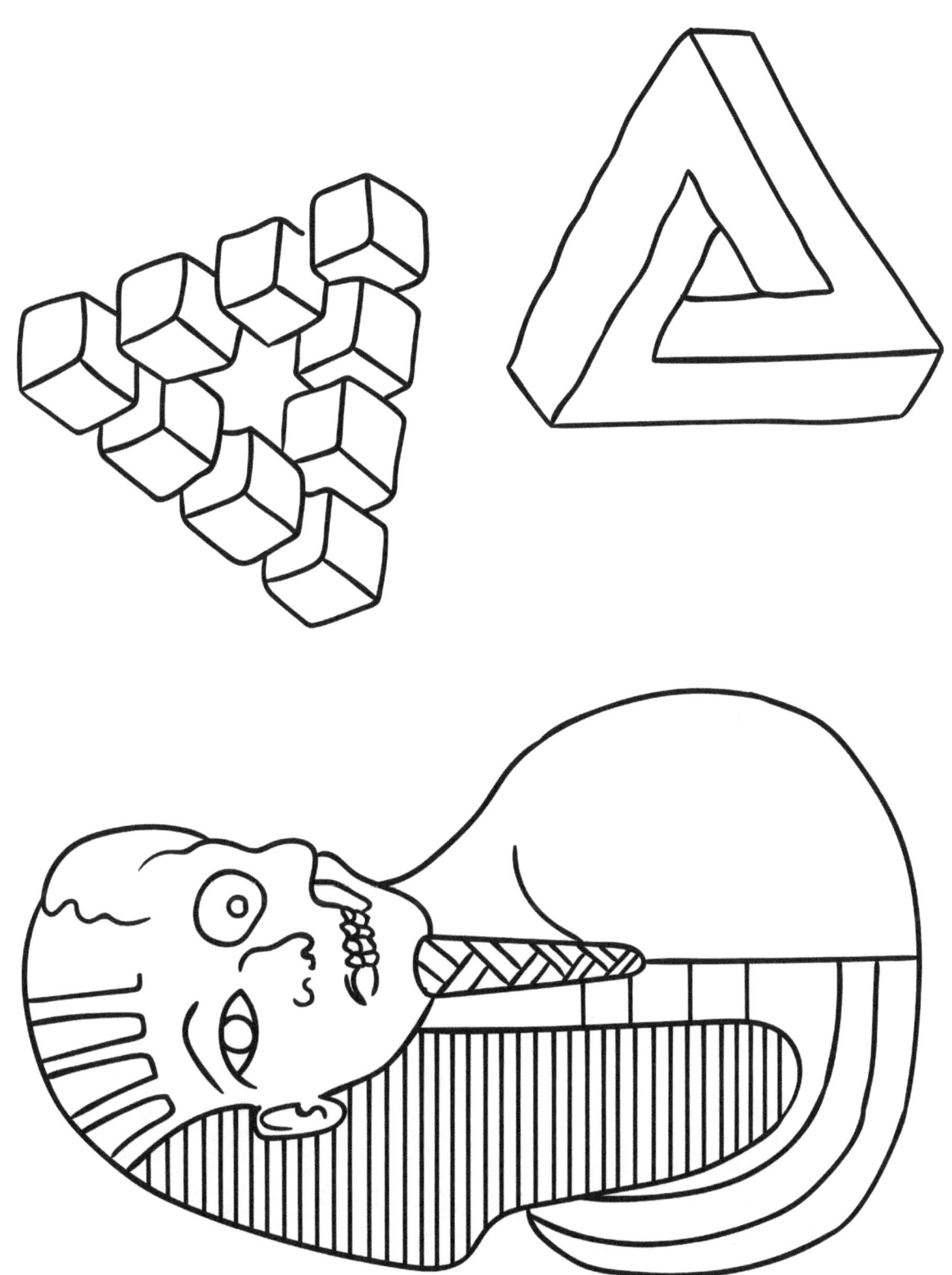

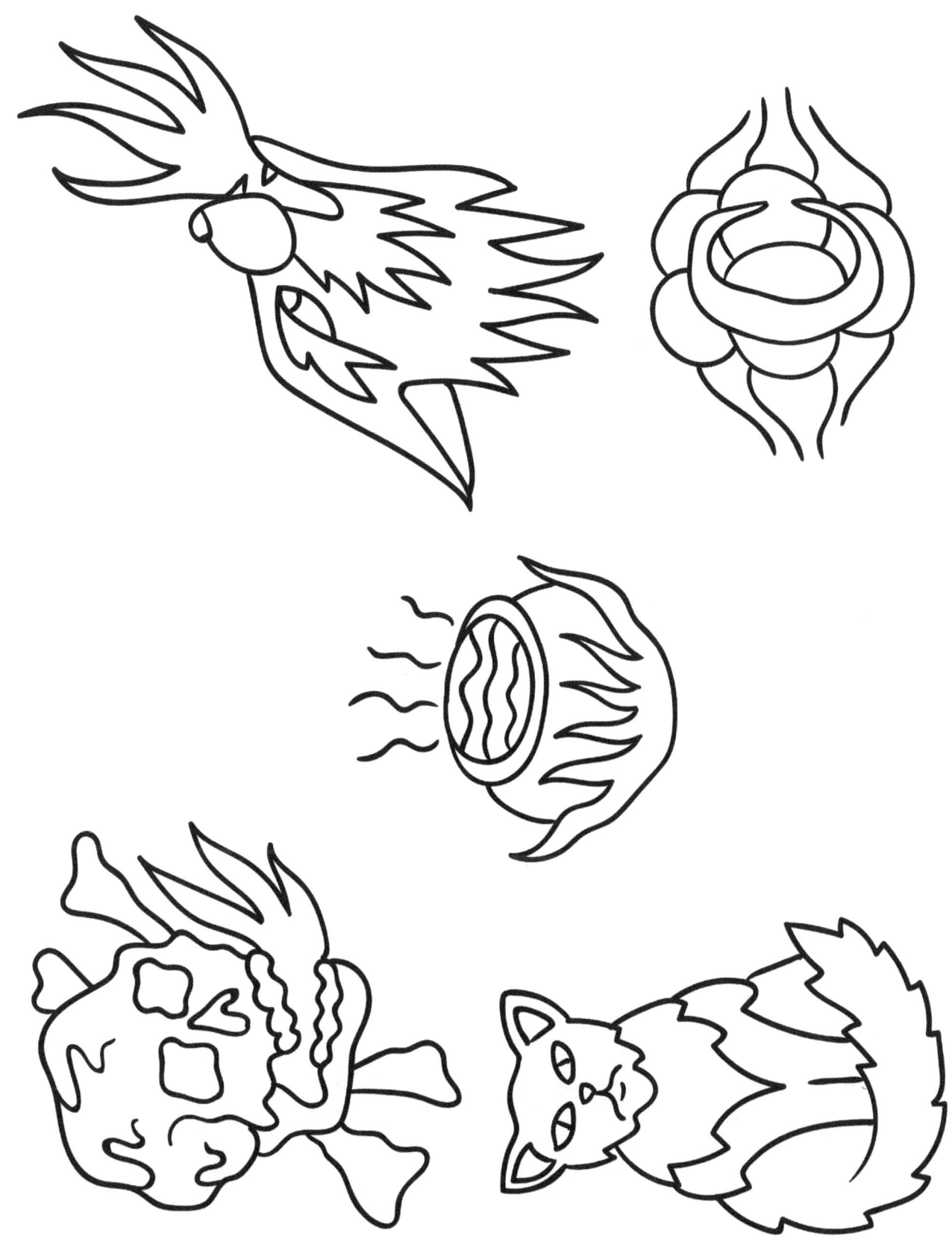

www.ingramcontent.com/pod-product-compliance
Lightning Source LLC
Chambersburg PA
CBHW080617180526
45168CB00007B/2945